THE FUTURE ORIENTATION OF THE YOUTH TODAY

BOSCO EKKA | SDB

ISBN 978-1-68523-817-9

Contents

Preface

Preface

It is said that youth are the future of the nation. Their orientation towards future is the land mark for the future of our society. Therefore, it very significant to know or analyse the future orientation as it gives the hint or direction for the future of the country. The Scholar work is focused on how do young people see the future. Are they optimistic or pessimistic? Do their views vary from culture to culture? Are young people actively engaged in creating their desired futures or are they passively receiving the future? What effect has globalization on youth culture? How is the future taught in schools? These and many other questions are dealt with in this research from around the Jorhat town, Assam, India on how youth see the future. Generally, youth are considered immature, irresponsible toward the future, impressionistic and dangerous toward self and others.

Most recently youth have become fodder for political speeches-they are the problem that reflects both the failure of the welfare state (dependence on the state), the failure of globalization (unemployment), and postmodernism (loss of meaning and the crisis of the spirit). Today, youth are seen not only as the problem, but equally as the force that can topple a regime. However, youth can also be seen as carriers of a new worldview, a new ideology.

This Study provides stimulating answers to questions about how youth see the future and their future roles. This research work will be of particular interest to scholars, students, researchers, and policymakers involved with youth issues and future studies.

The scholar work is based, on the interest of the researcher to comprehend future orientation of school going youth with reference to Jorhat town and contribute in bringing about revolutionize in orientation system and development in the society. There are studies done on the orientation towards future but the researcher has established no such study which has totally focused on school going youth as the contributing factor in the dynamics of change of the society. The researcher has used integrated approach of social science research in order to achieve a comprehensive understanding of the research study complementing the quantitative and qualitative approach all across the study course of action. The results and inferences of the area under discussion of study are done through the technique of triangulation convergence research design. The sampling size used for the quantitative data is 60, through the use of questionnaires as the tool for collecting information. The unstructured in depth interview is used as a tool to accumulate the data for the qualitative approach.

The research work begins with the introduction of the research where in the background of the study and the significance of the study is laid out; reviews the conceptualization of the study which is actually the literature related to the study either from books, websites, newspapers, journals, articles, magazines and other sources; the research methodology; the case narratives where the qualitative data is set out into checklist matrices for analysis; the analysis and interpretation of the collected facts. The analysis and interpretation is done with the help of the two approaches as result of comparing and contrasting the consequence of the approaches: compare and con-relate the two data sets and authenticate or expand the results of both the approaches. It trimmings with the presentation of the findings and suggestion of the research based on the analyzed data and the summary of the entire research.

I do wish that this study will enrich the readers with comprehensive understanding and information about the future orientation of school going youth.

Bosco Ekka

13/08/2021

Acknowledgements

Acknowledgments

Predominantly I humbly praise and thank the omnipresent God for the blessing and inspirations he has bestowed upon me during the study.

I express my sincere thanks to Dr. Jerry Thomas SDB, the director, Fr. Mathew C. Paul, the assistant director of Bosco Institute, Jorhat, for their support, encouragement and providing an ample opportunity to conduct the research project.

Appropriate supervision is one of the keys to success. I extend my boundless and everlasting thanks to my research supervisor Mr. Probin Topno, the faculty member of Bosco Institute. He took pain to go through all the pages to correct the necessities. The study would have remained incomplete without his timely assistance, direction and support for the completion of the study. I also acknowledge the contribution of Mrs. Manju, Mr. Joseph, Miss Pushpa and Mr. George for timely advice and suggestion. I furthermore thank all the staff members of the Institution.

I extend my heartfelt gratitude to Mr. Lal Das and Mr. Anand Kumar pal for their guidance and direction in SPSS. I am grateful to my parents, uncle, brothers and sister for their emotional and financial support. They had been with me in daily prayers for the accomplishment of my humble endeavour.

This project would have been incomplete without the support of my friends, classmates, the library staffs and the domestic workers. I would have stood defeated without their togetherness and friendly encouragement. With joy filled heart I thank each one of them. Finally, recognize the contribution of the good respondents without whom the study would have been impossible. I thank them for their open-handed cooperation and support.

Some people are able to foresee the future implications of their present behaviour. They understand how their present task-engagement is meaningfully related to desired future events and how their present behaviour serves the attainment of those future events. Other people would rather live in the present; they do not anticipate as strongly the future consequences of their present activities. The degree, to which people are able to look into the future, and thus foresee the usefulness of their present behaviour, differs from one person to another (Simons et al. 2004).

Future orientation refers to individuals' tendency to engage in thinking about the future (Seginer, 2009) and involves expectations, hopes, and fears (Nurmi, 1991; Markus & Nurius, 1986). It also is defined as the ability to anticipate future events (McCabe & Barnett, 2000). Research has shown that adolescents engage in thinking about the future and report future-oriented goals in a variety of life domains (Massey, Gebhardt, & Garnefski, 2008; Nurmi, 1991), including education and occupation (Lanz, Rosnati, Marta, & Scabini, 2001; Seginer, 1988), social relationships (Carroll, 2002), and money and financial stability (Budhwar, Reeves, & Farrell, 2000; Cohen & Cohen, 2001).

According to popular stereotype, young adolescents are notoriously short-sighted, oriented to the immediate rather than the future, unwilling or unable to plan ahead, and less capable than adults at envisioning the longer term consequences of their decisions and actions.

One of the characteristics of young youth is their almost unbelievably short time horizon. Given the choice between an ice cream cone now and a trip to Disney World in a month's time, many children will choose the ice cream cone. With maturity comes a willingness to postpone or forego pleasures for a future reward or a tolerance of present discomfort for the hope of future compensation. A future orientation is one of the most important evidences of transition into mature adulthood. The lower the degree of future orientation, the higher the sacrifice of future goods one is willing to make. As Banfield put it, "An individual's orientation toward the future will be regarded as a function of two factors, (1) ability to imagine a future, and (2) ability to discipline oneself to sacrifice present for future satisfaction." A future orientation may be seen in something as mundane as choosing to forego the dessert that might add to a waistline or contribute to health problems.

Statement of the problem

Rushdoony describes the future orientation of the society into four classes, "The upper class has a personal and broadly social future orientation. The middle class is similar, but of more restricted vision. The working class's future orientation is limited to very personal factors; a comfortable home, a new car, or the like. The lower class has no future orientation; he or she does not plan." We are told that we may learn from the ant, which provides in the summer for its winter needs. But we are becoming a society of the lower class, a society of short-sighted hedonists who are easily enticed away from productive work into temporary pleasures. Therefore, there is a great necessity to find cause and solution to the problem for better society and brighter nation.

The youth present an important population for investigating, as they exhibit a constellation of risky behaviour (Donovan, Jessor, & Costa, 1991; Morris et al., 1998), which has been theoretically linked to fundamental personality dispositions (Jessor,1998). Therefore, there is a great need to examine the linkages between personalities measures hypothesized to relate to future orientation. Stronger the linkages between personalities measures hypothesized and future orientation of youth brighter will be the future of a nation. Youth, particularly, is a time when impulsivity and sensation seeking, combined with a lack of orientation toward future consequences, are likely to be pronounced.

Orientation toward the future has been examined in relationship to present behaviours. Orientation toward the future as the degree to which individuals possess positive attitudes toward their futures includes perceiving a high degree of control over future outcomes in addition shows optimistic attitude towards their future domains of work, family, and social life. The ideas of being individuals who are pessimistic about their future are more likely to take risks with their health and safety. Put bluntly, a young person who believes that he or she may be dead by age 30 is unlikely to protect his or her long-term health and well-being.

Significant of the study

Future orientation is important for individuals' motivation and self-definition has been acknowledged by both psychologists (e.g., Bandura, 2001) and laypersons, as attested by the frequent use of future metaphors for promoting both commercial and public interests. Some of the areas of scientific inquiry, researchers have used different terms (e.g., future time orientation, future time perspective, possible selves) to refer to phenomena similar to those the researcher present here. Others have used "future orientation" to describe other non-thematic aspects of future-related issues, especially pertaining to extension (i.e., how far into the future individuals think) toward the future.

This study will examine the way one conceives of one's future is related to future events (carrier, family, decision making, etc). According to one's future orientation, one may plan certain activities in order to adapt to expected changes in the social environment. These expected and experienced changes, in turn, may cause changes in one's conception of the future. Future orientation is the capability to identify and interpret changes in the environment and trigger adequate responses to ensure long-term success that is endurance and sustainable.

To tackle the questions how youth become future oriented and thus ensure long-term vision and success in future. Some have done researchon foresightmethodssuch as scenario technique, Delphi analysis, etc., that allow us to explore the future, identify alternative futures or make predictions and others have worked on youthforesightas aprocess. These scholars imply that there is a youth foresight function, possible. It generates insights into the future and channels these to other social functions such as innovation management, strategic management, community development, marketing, or controlling. When we talk about youth future orientation we appreciate the capability to be build through a foresight that utilizes foresight methods.

Future orientation is the image individuals have regarding their future, as consciously represented and self-reported. Like autobiography, it tells a personal subjective life story consisting of those life domains individuals deem important, and gives meaning to one's life.

CHAPTER TWO

We are caught up in a paradox, one which might be called the paradox of conceptualization. The proper concepts are needed to formulate a good theory, but we need a good theory to arrive at the proper concepts.

• *Abraham Kaplan*

Introduction

In a research, review of literature is a vital component, it provide insight knowledge about the study, which is very important for a researcher to have clear knowledge of the study. The sources for review of literature will be researches, journals, and magazines, articles from the internet, newspapers and books.

Early Psychological Analyses

Early psychological analyses ofContemporary conceptualizations of future orientation can be traced back to early work of three psychologists: Frank (1939), Israeli (1930, 1936) and Lewin (1939, 1948). Their analyses addressed the conceptualization of future orientation as well as its motivational and developmental functions, especially addressing three issues: (a) Future orientation, or the construction of possible events and experiences in the future, is generated in the present, (b) Future orientation is domain specific and individuals construct their images of the future by relating to different domains, and (c) The content (themes) of these domains may be personal or social, realistic or ideal, and reality-based or fantastic.

For many developmental psychologists, adolescence is seen as a period of preparation for adulthood (Call, Reidel, Hein, McLoyd, Peterson, & Kipke, 2002). Underlying this perspective is the assumption that adolescents are being groomed and shaped, intentionally and unintentionally, for the roles they will take on in the future. Multiple systems are involved in this preparation and orientation, resulting in a complex process which operates to propel adolescents toward thinking about and making plans for later adult attainments. Through this process, adolescents should gain experiences that help them shape their own expectations of the future, which include perceptions of possibilities and opportunities (Nurmi, 2004). These expectations will impact their decisions and the opportunities they pursue, placing them on trajectories that shape the rest of their lives. However, there is little theoretical clarity and cohesion with regard to the construct of future orientation or the processes involved in developing and shaping an adolescent's orientation toward the future.

A number of constructs have been of interest for decades in exploring young people's connection to the wider community, including prosaically orientation, civic engagement, participation in organized youth activities, and volunteerism/community service. For example, many of the themes of the current discussion about youth civic engagement are found in the youth participation or youth as resources movement of late 1960s-early 1980s (Kleinbard, 1997).

Youth participation then was defined as the chance for young people to engage in "responsible, challenging action that meets genuine needs, with opportunity for planning and decision making affecting others..." (Kleinbard, 1997). Youth engagement in the life of the community traditionally has been seen as a critical aspect of healthy development. Such engagement may be expressed in terms of "unselfish acts of caring and kindness" Haynes & Comer, 1997, p. 79), or described as civic activism that addresses societal problems and works toward social change (Wheeler, 2002).

Contributing to community betterment through helping others may be a sign of young people's emerging civic competence. At the same time, however, it is an important means for "youth to develop their identity...not as a self-enclosed individual achievement, but rather as a social identification that transcends a given moment in time" (Youniss, Bales, Christmas-Best, Diversi, McLaughlin, & Silbereisen, 2002). That is, in helping to get together the needs of others than themselves, young people start to think of.

Youth

Youth is best understood as a period of transition from the dependence of childhood to adulthood's independence. That's why, as a category, youth is more fluid than other fixed age-groups. Yet, age is the easiest way to define this group, particularly in relation to education and employment, because 'youth' is often referred to a person between the ages of leaving compulsory education, and finding their first job.

The idea of 'youth' came up in the 20[th]century, when Keniston, a psychologists (1970) proposed a new 'life phase', which he called 'youth' to mark the gap, increased by number of years of adolescence of the 19[th]century. (Morgan, King, Weisz, and schopler, 2008) The defining typology in the discourse of what it means to be a young person. Youth is time of transition to adulthood, from dependence to independence. Therefore, youth-hood is a specific cognitive, psychological, physical period of growth. It is a time when the wind is getting wired and forming impressions of the world. (Patel, Venkateswaran, Prakash, and Shekar, 2013).

Youth is the time of life when one is young, but often means the time between childhoodand adulthood(maturity). Definitions of the specific age range that constitutes youth vary. An individual's actual maturity may not correspond to their chronologicalage, as immature individuals can exist at all ages. Youth research has come to define youth through personal experience, especially in terms of an individual's level dependency, which can be marked in various ways according to different cultural perspectives. Personal experience is marked by an individual's cultural norms or traditions while a youth's level of dependency refers to the extent to which they still rely on their family emotionally and economically. Youth is also defined as "the appearance, freshness, vigour, spirit, etc., characteristic of one who is young".

The United Nations, for statistical purposes, defines 'youth', as those persons between the ages of 15 and 24 years, without prejudice to other definitions by Member States. The Secretary-General first referred to the current definition of youth in 1981 in his report to the General Assembly on International Youth Year (A/36/215, Para. 8 of the annex) and endorsed it in ensuing reports (A/40/256, Para. 19 of the annex). However, in both the reports, the Secretary-General also recognized that, apart from that statistical definition, the meaning of the term 'youth' varies in different societies around the world. When the General Assembly, by its resolution 50/81 in 1995, adopted the World Programme of Action for Youth to the Year 2000 and beyond, it reiterated that the United Nations defined youth as the age collection of 15-24 years.

Time perspective:

Time is the valuable resource and one of greatest gift nature has given us. It is not given to us all at once , it is parcelled out bit by bit, moment by moment, it is divided into years, months, days , hours, minutes, seconds and even fraction of seconds. People's attitude towards time is complex and variable.

Educated Youth

Usually educated youth means intellectually, morally, and socially instructed person. For the Researcher 'educated youth' means youth who are studying in their higher secondary. Youth is a period of student-hood. The youth today are no less valiant. They need to be oriented to face the future demands of the modern world.

Needs of youth

Youth is like spring, and over raised season. Youth are people, with the basic needs like all people such as food, sexual outlet, clothing, shelter, as well as love, recognition, inner fulfilment. Biologically, the need for a sexual outlet is great, and psychologically, sociologically, the need to come to terms with one's view of human relations is vast. Youth is the time when one begins to search for defining oneself as different from those with whom one has been close to. There is an intensive need for experimentation among youth.

Decision making

It is the whole process by which minds are made up, the mental movements which leads to decisions, in a word it is 'thinking'. It is the kind of thinking that leads to action. Decision making pattern implies choice from several or many possibilities. Thinking is the preliminary work of weighing up the pros and cons for each course of action.

Decision making is the study of identifying and choosing alternatives based on the values and preferences of the decision makers. Making a decision implies that there are alternative choices to be considered like the highest probability of success or effectiveness and best fit with our goals, desire, lifestyles, values, and so on.

Decision making can be defined as the process of making choices among possible alternatives. The skills considered important to effective decision making are based on a normative model of decision making, which prescribes how decisions should be made. These skills include: 1) identifying the possible options; 2) identifying the possible consequences that follow from each option; 3) evaluating the desirability of each of the consequences; 4) assessing the likelihood of each consequence; and 5) making a choice using a "decision rule" (Furby & Beyth-Marom, 1992). In a model for teaching decision making, Wilson & Kirby (1984) include the following skills: defining the decision to be made; educating oneself (gathering facts and generating alternatives); considering options; identifying a choice; designing a plan to carry out the decision; and evaluating the decision. These models address goal-directed, plan full decision making. Although cognitive aspects of decision making are considered important to adolescent risk-taking (Lavery, Siegel, Cousins & Rubovits, 1993), risk-related decisions require additional considerations (Furby & Beyth-Marom, 1992).

The saying 'Practice makes a man perfect', the more we apply this principles of our choice the better we get at making better decision and the faster it progress.We must ensure that all available model are used effectively because the nine model is the tricky one and let us choose options, strategy and between option. This will prepare people for the fact that, when they sometimes are making bad decision.

Change

No matter how old are a person is, at some time he or she will be pulled, pushed, or prodded by pain to leave his or her comfort zone and move along a path from the land of wish and want, through a gate that leads to the land of will do.

Career

Career is an occupation undertaken for a significant period of a person's life and with opportunities for progress. It is the progressand actionstaken by a person throughout a lifetime, especially those related to that person'soccupations. A career is often composed of the jobs held, title earned and work accomplished over a long period of time, rather than just referring to one position.Career is defined by the oxford English dictionaryas a person's "course or progress through life (or a distinct portion of life)". In this definition career is understood to relate to a range of aspects of an individual's life, learning and work. Career is also frequently understood to relate to the working aspects of an individual's life. The other way in which the term career is used to describe an 'occupation' or a 'profession' that usually involves special training or formal education, and is considered to be a person's lifework.

Future career orientation is nothing but setting one's sights to recognise one's likes and dislikes, identifies ones priorities, understanding of core values and pulling it all together. It also imply understanding ones talents recalling the accomplishments, appraise of honesty, getting a second opinion. It is orienting self to make things happen by taking one step at a time, identifying constrains, getting one's own way. It is a boosting of one's skills, overcoming obstacles and making a successful move.

Focus

It is one of the essential elements of high degree of future orientation of youth. "Where am I headed?" one ask oneself. Lacking of focus can lead to quick frustration. This focus helps to set goals each year, each month, and even each week. Focus is powerful because it forces one to filter; one instinctively evaluate whether or not a particular action will help one move toward ones goal. It can be powerful tools for the youth of today to have future orientation.

Family

In the most basic definition, a group of people who share a legal bond or a blood bond is a family. Orientation of a family is where everyone experiences love, understanding, warmth and friendship. It is a place where there is more togetherness, greater concern and love for one another. It is institution where its members have faith in one another, where there is unity in spite of differences of opinion, shortcomings and failure.

Legal Bonds: Families are legally bound through marriages, adoptions, and guardianships, including the rights, duties, and obligations of those legal contracts. Legal bonds can be changed, expanded, or dissolved to change the composition of a family.

Blood Bonds: Individuals who are directly related through a common ancestor are part of a family. This includes both close and distant relatives such as siblings, parents, grandparents, aunts, uncles, nieces, nephews, and cousins. Researching a family tree or genealogical records can reveal familial blood bonds. Despite the apparent simplicity of this definition of family, the idea of family goes far beyond just legal or blood relationships for many people. There are many different types of families, each of which is equally viable as a supportive, caring unit. Some of them are nuclear family, extended family, complex family, step family, traditional family, adopted family, foster family etc...

Rationale of the study

The purpose of this study is to evaluate how educated think about their future, and how that is related to other aspects of student life. To evaluate how educated youth think about their future, and how that is related to other aspects of life. To help the society to analyse in what direction the youth of today are heading to. To provide ground for society in setting goals, planning, exploring option and making commitments that guide a person's behaviour and developmental course. Researchers know that people think about their futures, but little is known about how different events of future-oriented thinking are related, or how that affects identity and other areas of cognitive and social development. This study is not intended to provide any personal benefit to you, but it will benefit society as we learn more about how people think about and conceptualize their futures.

CHAPTER THREE

Introduction

Methodology is a systematically study to solve the research problem. It is a science of study how a fact can be proved scientifically. It gives an idea of how the study deals with the particular problem using various methods and techniques. It is important not only to know how to use research methods but also the logic behind the methods used in the context of the study of a specific topic. It gives the explanation of using a particular method or technique. Research results are capable of evaluation either by the study himself or even by others. The knowledge of methodology provides the study to do better research by developing disciplined thinking or a 'bend of mind' to observe or treat the data. It helps in forming the objectives of the study.

In this study, in order to understand the future orientation of college going youth, the researcher used integrated approach which is the combination of both quantitative and qualitative research approaches. The researcher has used family, decision making and career to understand the degree to which youth are able to look into their future.

Research design

Research design is a blue print of the research. In this study, the orientation, towards future of the college going youth, have been studied based on the property-disposition character. Therefore, in this study, the researcher has taken "the convergence triangulation" method as the research design.

The triangulation research is an integrated research approach design includes the strategies and tactics, one selects in carrying out research studies. Designing such an integrated research design primarily depends very much on the topic of research studies, objectives of the research and research questions the researcher had tried to answer. It is a detail plan of research study explaining how the research is carried out by using both quantitative and qualitative approaches. It described about the research questions is answered by each research approach, focal of the study, sampling methods and techniques of data collection and analysis of data.

The most common and well known integrated research design is the triangulation design which is used to understand the research problem comprehensively by obtaining complimentary date using quantitative and qualitative approach on the same topic of research.

Triangulation convergence design of triangulation method of integrated approach is used when a researcher wishes to directly compare and contrast quantitative approach research findings and statistical inference with qualitative approach findings. The objective in using this research is to draw together be differing strengths and weaknesses of quantitative approach research with those of qualitative approach research.

This research design is used to understand the research problem comprehensively by obtaining different but complementary data using quantitative and qualitative approach on the same topic of research. The triangulation research design is a one-phase research design in which researchers use quantitative and qualitative approaches during the sametimeframe and give equal weight to both the approaches. The triangulation research design is also called the "concurrent triangulation design"because the research study is completed by using quantitative approach and qualitative approach simultaneously. By and large, it involves the simultaneous, but separate, collection and analysis of quantitative and qualitative data so that the researcher may best understand the phenomenon under study.

In this research design two sets of data- quantitative and qualitative is collected simultaneously and analyzed independently. The result of quantitative and qualitative is merged, normally by comparing, contrasting and interpreting the results. Inferences are drawn on the basis of the result of quantitative and qualitative researches giving equal weight to both the approaches. The procedure of triangulation convergence research design is diagrammatically presented in the below figure.

Collection of quantitative data.

Analyses of quantitative data.

Result of quantitative data.

Inferences are made by integrating result of both quantitative and qualitative.

Compare and contrast both the result.

Collection of qualitative data.

Analysis of qualitative data.

Result of qualitative data.

FIG: CONVERGENCE TRIANGULATION METHOD

Main objective of the study

To study the degree to which youth are able to look into the future and the images individuals hold concerning their future.

Specific objective of the study

1. To study the future carrier orientation of school going youth.
2. To understand the decision making pattern for future of youth.
3. To study future orientation of school going youth towards family.

Hypothesis

Hypothesis is the assumption of the researcher on the topic of study which is to be subjected to scientific testing to prove its validity under the given circumstances. Hence, the researcher had framed the following hypotheses according to his area of study.

1. H1= There is an association between age and level of future family orientation.

   H0=There is no association between the age and level of future family orientation.

2. H2= There is an association between future planning and decision making.

   H0= There is no association between future planning and decision making.

3. H3= There is a relationship between time perspective and decision making.

   H0= There is no relationship between decision making and time perspective.

Research questions

1. Area of interest
2. Decision in daily activity

3. Influence in making decision
4. Family interest
5. Independency in daily life
6. Concept of future
7. Short term and long term goals
8. Time perspective

Sampling

Sampling is the process of selecting the smallest appropriate representation of the entire population by means of scientific techniques. If the sample of the study is appropriate, the chances of acquiring new scientific information about the phenomenon of study and the formulation of theory about the phenomenon in the new changed scenario would be more acceptable.

Sampling universe

Sampling universe of the study is the college going students of standard from XI to graduation of age group from fifteen to twenty five.

Sampling technique

In integrated research, the stratified purposeful sampling is the combination of stratified sampling (a probability sampling) and purposive sampling (a non-probability sampling). It is used when the researcher wishes to ensure that certain research participants varying on preselected parameters are included in the study. The researcher assumed youth as the important part in society in this study (D.K. Lal Das, 2013).

Sampling period

Sampling period is taken as one month during the study (1stto 30thJanuary, 2015).

Sampling size

Minimum 60 respondents for the quantitative data collection and number researched for qualitative data collection is based on the principle of divergence and saturation point.

Inclusion and Exclusion criteria

Inclusion criteria

All school going youth both boys and girls, between the age group of 15 to 25, who are regular students are in the inclusion criteria of the research.

Exclusion criteria

Individuals as boys and girls who are pursuing their study in any medium other than English are in the exclusion criteria of the research.

Theoretical and operational definition

Educated Youth: Educated youth can be instrumental in shaping and directing a society to a bright future (Mammen Mathew, 2013).

Decision making: Decision making is the process of identifying and selecting a course of action to solve a specific problem (John Adair, 1985).

Family: A group of people who share a legal bond or a blood bond is a family (http://family.lovetoknow.com).

Career: Career is the progressand actionstaken by a person throughout a lifetime, especially those related to that person'soccupations(Rob Yeung, 2002).

Future orientation: Future orientation refers to individuals' tendency to engage in thinking about the future (Seginer, 2009) and involves expectations, hopes, and fears (Nurmi, 1991).

Operational definition: Operational definition is the presentation of the understanding of the variables and concepts that the researcher is dealing with in the particular study in accordance with the context of the study.

Future orientation: Future orientationis the degree to which an individual visualises oneself as engaging in making decision about his or her career and family which yet to come.

Family: Family a man and a woman united in marriage, together with children is called family.

Educated youth: Educated youth is all those who are undergoing academic training in higher secondary and belong to the age group of 15 to 25 years.

Career: Career is an occupation undertaken for a significant period of a person's life and with opportunities for progress.

Procedure

In this study, the primary data for the quantitative analysis was collected using questionnaire which is prepared in a language understood by the researcher's respondents. As the researcher meets his respondents in the research setting, after getting the consent of the respondent to be a participant in providing the research information, the questionnaires were administered to them by the researcher personally and the data were collected on the spot. The quantitative data of the research is subjected to SPSS for further analysis while the qualitative data collected using in depth unstructured interview. Each interview was treated as individual case study which is subjected to cross checking and coding finally to reach "field based theory". The secondary required data of the research collected from magazines, journals, news papers, and internet.

Conclusion

The researcher has selected the methodology for the integrated study of future orientation of youth which involves the appropriated research design, sampling process and procedure of conducting the research. Research methodology is an indispensible ingredient of any research which speaks volume of the accuracy of data collection and the analysis followed. Keeping this in mind, the researcher has chosen convergence triangulation integrated research design and stratified purposeful sampling for accessing data from the field.

Introduction

Integrated approach studies require the use of both tools of data collection that are commonly associated with quantitative and qualitative research, such as in –depth unstructured interview and standardised scales and structured questionnaires respectively. When target phenomenon can be observed, observations of behaviour and physical environment are used to obtain more unbiased data in qualitative approach. In integrated research approach qualitative and qualitative data sets are interlinked, preserving the numbers and words in each set. Alternatively, data are transformed to create one data set, with qualitative data converted into quantitative data or vice versa. Interlinking the results of qualitative and quantitative analysis is accomplished by treating each data set with the techniques usually used with that data ; that is quantitative techniques are used to analyse quantitative data and qualitative techniques are used to analyse qualitative data. Constant comparison and qualitative data narrative analysis techniques are used to analyse interview data, whereas one or more statistical techniques are used to analyse data from research instruments in quantitative approach. The result of quantitative analysis of quantitative data and qualitative analysis of qualitative data then integrated in the interpretive level of research but stand independently. In convergence triangulation method, the integration of data is being done by merging both the results of the analysis connecting the two data sets by having one builds on the other.

Quantitative approach

In this study, the researcher has tried to understand future orientation of educated youth by using both quantitative and qualitative methods. The analysis data of quantitative approach is listed below.

TABLE 1

Responses

Distribution of Responses

Frequency

Percentages

17

42

70

16

12

20

18

6

10

Total

60

100

AGE OF THE RESPONDENTS

The table 1 shows the ages of the youth who participated in the research process. There are majority of the youth who fall under the age 17, very less fall under the age 16 and a handful of youth are of 18 years of age. So there is one category of youth with different age. So, we can say that all the respondents are form age group of 16 to 18 ages.

TABLE 2

SEX OF THE RESPONDENTS

Responses

Distribution of Responses

Frequency

Percentages

Male

22

36.7

Female

38

63.3

Total

60

100.0

The table 2 represents the distribution of sex among the respondent. It shows majority as the female and rest male in the research participants.

TABLE 3

DECISION MAKING PATTERN

Responses

Distribution of Responses

Frequency

Percentages

Low

18

30.0

Moderate

27

45.0

High

15

25.0

Total

60

100.0

The table 3 represents the pattern of orientation towards decision making of youth in frequency and percentages. The table shows a good number youth are having average orientation towards the decision making pattern. This implies that a good number of the youth follow certain patterns that are neither extraordinarily high nor low future orientation in decision making. So, we can say that a fairly good number of youth have, to some extent an averagely effective decision making pattern. As the future orientation also implies future vision we can say that very low percentages of youth have a good future orientation towards decision making pattern. Again, there are also a handful youth who have limited future orientation towards decision making pattern.

TABLE 4
ORIENTATION TOWARDS FUTURE PLANNING

Responses

Distribution of Responses

Frequency

Percentages

Low

16

26.7

Moderate

31

51.7

High

13

21.7

Total

60

100.0

The table 4 is the presentation of future orientation towards planning in percentages of youth today. From the frequency and percentages it can be said that good majority of youth have average future orientation towards planning or has a tendency to engage in thinking about future and involves expectation and hopes but in a limited manner. Again, the lowest percentages of youth have a very good orientation towards future planning. But we cannot deny the fact that there are many youth who have poor orientation towards future planning.

TABLE 5
ORIENTATION TOWARDS TIME PERSPECTIVE

Responses

Distribution of Responses

Frequency

Percentages

Low

18

30.0

Moderate

29

48.3

High

13

21.7

Total

60

100.0

The table 5 signifies the future orientation of youth towards time perspective in the form of frequency and percentages. It shows a good majority of the youth having an average rate in future orientation towards time perspective. Thus, it can be interpreted that a very good majority care their future or often think of time that yet to come but it is limited to certain extend. Again, there are a very few youth who has very good orientation towards time perspective and a handful youth have very poor orientation towards time perspective.

TABLE 6

ORIENTATION TOWARDS FUTURE CAREER

Responses

Distribution of Responses

Frequency

Percentages

Low

16

26.7

Moderate

31

51.7

High

13

21.7

Total

60

100.0

The table 6 denotes the degree of future orientation of youth towards career in a frequency and percentages form. The table imply that a majority of youth have and think very often about their career. This also means that a good many youth visualises their future career. So, it can be said that the future orientation towards career among majority of youth is moderate with a limited vision. Again, a very less number of youth have high orientation towards future Career and a few who are with very low orientation towards future career.

TABLE 7

FUTURE ORIENTATION TOWARDS FAMILY LIFE

Responses

Distribution of Responses

Frequency

Percentages

Low

18

30.0

Moderate

29

48.3

High

13

21.7

Total

60

100.0

The table 7 represents percentages of youth with their future orientation towards family life. The table shows that a good number of youth has family orientation moderately to certain extend and on the other hand a handful of youth has high orientation towards family life. Beside these there are a group of youth who are little less than averages have very poor future orientation towards their family life.

TABLE 8
ASSOCIATION BETWEEN DECISION MAKING PATTERN AND FUTURE PLANNING

Decision making pattern

Future planning

Total

Low

moderate

high

Low

8

(13.3%)

7

(11.7%)

3

(5.0%)

18 (30.0%)

Moderate

5

(8.3%)

19

(31.7%)

3

(5.0%)

27 (45.0%)

High

3

(5.0%)

5

(8.3%)

7 (11.7%)

15 (25.0%)

Total

16 (26.7%)

31

(51.7%)

13

(21.7%)

60 (100%)

x2=12.351   **df = 4 P = 0.015**

The table 8 represents the cross tabulation of the decision making pattern and future planning of the youth.

The Chi-square test conducted for decision making pattern and future planning shows the significance value P = 0.015 which is less than the limit of significance value 0.05. Therefore, there is an association between decision making pattern and future planning of youth.

TABLE 9
ASSOCIATION BETWEEN DECISION MAKING PATTERN AND TIME PERSPECTIVE

Decision making pattern

time perspective

Total

Low

moderate

High

Low

5

(8.3%)

11

(18.3%)

2
(3.3%)
18
(30.0%)
Moderate
13
(21.7%)
11
(18.3%)
3
(5.0%)
27
(45.0%)
High
0
(0.0%)
7
(11.7%)
8 (13.3%)
15
(25.0%)
Total
18
(30%)
29
(48.3%)
13 (21.7%)
60
(100%)

x2=17.689   df = 4 P = 0.001

The table 9 represents the cross tabulation of decision making pattern and time perspective level of youth.

The Chi-Square test result shows the P value as 0.001 which is lower than the significance value of .05. Hence there is an association between decision making pattern and level of time perspective of youth.

TABLE 10

ASSOCIATION BETWEEN AGE AND FUTURE ORIENTATION OF FAMILY LIFE

Age

Family
Total
Low
Moderate
High
16.00
4
(6.7%)
6
(10.0%)
2
(3.3%)
12
(20.0%)
17.00
13
(21.7%)
23
(38.3%)
6
(10.0%)
42
(70.0%)
18.00
1
(1.7%)
0
(0.0%)
5
(8.3%)
6
(10.0%)
Total
18
(30.0%)

29

(48.3%)

13 (21.7%)

60

(100%)

$x2=15.404$ df = 4 P = .004

The table 10 represents the cross tabulation of age and future orientation towards family life of youth.

The Chi-Square test result shows the P value as 0.004 which is lower than the significance value of .05. Hence there is an association between age and future orientation towards family life of youth.

Qualitative approach

Introduction

In this integrated research study, the researcher puts his effort to understand future orientation of school going youth. Here in depth understanding of future orientation of youth is measured using qualitative approach. The researcher has chosen the school going youth for collecting in depth data through case study. This approach will help the researcher to avoid some of the problems of quantitative approach.

Case narratives

The researcher used in-depth unstructured interview. The data collected from the stakeholders are noted down. Here the data collected through in depth unstructured interview is transformed into case narrative in accordance to the area of study mentioned in the methodology.

Case 1

Ravi (name changed) age 17 studying in Don Bosco School Bagchung, Jorhat. He has one younger brother and younger sister; both are perusing schooling. His parents are alive and doing very well in life. Mother is a house wife and father is a business person. His father runs small grocery store in the town.

He said that he is in 12thstandard and is quite good in studying. He said that though he is good in studies he does not plan for study activities systematic manner. His studies and daily activities depend on his feelings. Now and then he plans his study and other activities but very often he fails to carry out the plan. Therefore, he is not interested in making plan. He thinks making plan is a waste of time.

He has many friends in the school and also at home. He has very limited friends among the opposite sex. He also scares of falling in love with girls and tends to avoid their company. He has seen student ruining their studies after falling in love. So he is quite careful about this matter. He thinks that falling in love will lead him to marriage before he could accomplish his studies.

When he was asked about his thought on marriage he said that marriage is out of his mind as per now. He said that getting marriage and establishing family is the work of the person who has job security and has secure future. He will see later when to get marry. He hardly imagines his future marriage or family life.

He said that now he is only focusing on study and doing engineering after class 12. He is seriously now preparing for his coming exam. After exam he will go for coaching class for the engineering entrance exam. But he is not sure what he will do after engineering. He only said, "Let's see what happen". He is quite clear about his short term goal but long term goal is in question mark.

When he was asked how he decided to go for engineering, he said that he is advised and guided by his parents to choose the career for sustainable future. He also thinks that it is not a bad option to earn and be happy in life. He said that independently he finds difficult to make decision and as a result his decision in daily life is mostly influenced by his friends and class mate.

Besides studying he is interested in games and music. He always tries to find some time to play games. He thinks that games refreshes his mind and he could study better than when he does not play. He also loves to spend time with his friends.

Case 2

Ram (name changed) is a student studying in class XII. He is 18 years old. He has his parents and two sisters. His father is working in government sector. He belongs to middle class family. He is quite good in studies. He is very much participative in the class. His parent always motivates him to study and participate in extra curriculum activities. He is also very much interested in games. His favourite games are football and volleyball. His favourite subject is biology and math.

He wants to be engineer in the future if everything in life goes well. He is not sure whether his interests have any relationship with the career he wants to take up in the future. But he believes that everything in life is interconnected and everything he does will help him to live either unhappy or happy life in the future. He wishes to take engineering as career because he has seen people with engineering doing very well in life and earning a lot.

He says once he gets job after qualifying in the profession he will think of settling down or establish his own family. He prefers love marriage thought marriage is not in his mind as now. Even his parents use to tell him that this is the time only think about studies and career and he is advised to focus on studies and career.

He is a busy very often due to the assignments and other personal activity. Though he has many things in the mind to carry out and he does carry out but not formal or perfect way. He said that he does not have fixed plan for daily life. He has plan but not rigid plan for future. Now and then he things of his future but he is not really determined to achieve his future plan. He believes in living today than living tomorrow which no one is sure about.

Sometime he thinks about his career and makes effort to gather information related to his career. He sometime does dedicate time thinking about future within the daily activity. He does not spent much time before carrying out any task. He makes decision in life without much bothering about the future. He said that most often his decisions in daily life are influenced by his relatives, friend and parents.

Case 3

Prakash (name changed) is a class 12 student studying in English medium higher secondary school. He is 17 years old tall and handsome boy. He has his parents and one younger sister. His father is working as a teacher in one of the government school. His younger sister is studying in the school where his father is a teacher. Mother is house wife as well as run small shop which attached to their house.

He is a very serious in studies and honest boy from small time but hardly participates in school activities. He is quite shy to talk with others especially with the girls of his age group. In every class he carries good marks. He took science stream in his higher secondary level. He says support from his parents, encouragement and positive attitude of his parents towards him help to improve studies.

Now he is even more confident with his studies as well as his goal for which he wishes to make a move after higher secondary. He is quite clear about his next step after the final exam. He wants to pass higher secondary and join Indian army, substituting his father, and then he will go through training before starting the job.

When he was asked about establish his own family in the future he said, "I don't believe in love marriage." He has seen family bond with love marriage has been shattered. He has lost faith on love marriage by seeing various broken family which once upon a time had love marriage. Though marriage is not in his mind at that time, later on he wishes to have arranged marriage. He finds best example for successful arrange marriage is his own parents.

Again, when he was asked about how he makes decision, he said, "Whenever I need to make major decision, for instance for choosing the stream for doing my higher secondary education, I always consult my parents and also my parents." For other thing in life he never makes any decision or plan to carry out daily task. Most of the time, he does what he feels and thinks best at that moment.

Beside his studies and other daily activities he has developed a very liking towards games. He likes football and is quite good in that. He also thinks that his interest games will help him in his career as he has plan to join India army where physical activities like game has one of the major role.

Case 4

Sujata (name changed) is studying in class XII. She is 17 years old. Her parents are alive. Her mother is a house wife and father has government service. She has one sister studying in class X and one brother perusing study in Bachelor of Science, first year.

After her matriculation she was given chance to choose the stream of study which would take up for her further studies. She independently decided to study in Science stream. She is good in studies. Her favourite subject is physics. She also hopes to do well in the final higher secondary examination.

She likes to study science. Therefore, after class XII she wants to continue science studies by doing her B.sc in chemistry. She said, "I don't want take physics though I like because I think afterwards physics will be tough in B.sc level."

When she was asked about what career to take up in the future, she said, "I have not plan anything for the future." She has not planned anything for her future. She has no idea what she will do after studies. She has not thought of what career to take up in the future.

Planning ahead for any activities is not her way of doing things. She does not even plan what book to study at what time. She just does what she thinks needed at that moment. She does not find the need of planning.

She says family is one of the important aspects of her life. She gives credit for her success to her family member who understood and support all through her life so far. Though she cherishes family life she has not thought about or not dreamed about of having her own family in the future. She said, "In future if I have to marry I would go for love marriage rather than arranged marriage whereby I will have pre-understanding of life partner whom I spending whole life rising up a good family."

On the factor of decision making she said, "I do not make decision consciously very often. I decide as things come in my life. Beside this most of the time my decision depends on others like my parents and family member." She is not very much aware about her decision making process.

Beside her study and other daily activities she likes to read novels. Whenever she is alone she reads novel and other books. She also enjoys listening music. Sometime she tends to spend more time in reading novel than reading her academic study books.

Case 5

Sunil (name changed) is a 16 years student studying in class XI. His parents are alive. His mother is a house wife and father is farmer. He has only one brother who is doing his study in second year Bachelor of Arts. His parents are very encouraging and supportive in the matters of their studies though his parents are not educated or had no chance to attend schooling. He enjoys good relationship with his brother and parents. Parents have lots of trust in him.

Sunil is very much ambitious person. He said, "I want to be Deputy Commissioner but I don't know what are the studies required for the career." He makes effort to gather information related to the career from different people like teachers, friends etc. He is confident about pursuing his career. He makes lots of effort, keeps working at difficult, because he believes that all these things will help him to fulfil his ambition.

He has lots of faith on his uncle and aunty as they are educated. He always consults them and asks for opinion before making any major decision. He says he used to think lots before making any decision. He quite independent to decide what is best for him. Parents do not interfere much in whatever he does except asking why he is doing what he is doing.

His economic condition is not very good. He wants finish higher secondary and do any part time job and continue his higher studies. He is ready for any kind of work which will help him to accomplish his ambition.

He is very hard working person.

When he was enquired about his marriage and having his own family he said, "I have given no thoughts to marriage and having my family. I find very difficult to thing about this due to my present situation."

Though ambition minded he has no fixed and proper plan to execute or reach or accomplish his ambition. He hardly practices planning when he does something. He says he does no how make plan and execute it. He consciously never did this.

Case 6

Bornali (name changed) is a 19 years student studying in class XII. She is good in studies and also in dance. Her favourite subject is biology. Her parents are doing well in life. Her mother is nurse and father is business person. She is very beautiful with average height. She has one brother and two sisters. She is the youngest among all. As she is the youngest among all siblings she gets lots of affection and love from her parents and also from her brother and sisters.

She finds herself very lucky because she gets lots of freedom and support and encouragement from all the members of the family in her studies and in the things she wants to do. After the higher secondary examination she wishes to continue her studies in a profession study of paramedical. She thinks and feels that that is the right and fitting vocation or occupation which she could carry out happily with lots of satisfaction in life.

She always found herself from childhood onwards in the environment where she could think and choose for herself. Even now as youth she found herself independent to decided and plan to give entrance exam for paramedical studies. Parents gave no objection to her decision; in fact they were glad that she made her own choice for life without being pressurised from any external force.

When she was encouraged to talk about her plan on having own family she said, "I am still young and do not want to get involve in family business so fast. Let me work after finishing my professional course for some time, then I will see good person whom I find worthy to be my life partner." So far she did not find any pressure from parents for getting married. She strongly believe that her parents will support her in whatever decision she makes in the matters of marriage and settling down to establish her own family.

In free time she likes to do painting beside her serious studies and other activities of daily life. She finds pleasure in painting and encouragement when people admire her painting. Beside all these she also likes to hang out with her friends, window shopping etc.

Case 7

Niraj (name changed) is a student of class XII. He is 16 years old tell with fair complexion. His parents are alive. Father is a business person and mother is lecturer in one of the college. He is the only sibling in the family. The economic condition of the family is very good. From childhood onwards he is interested in electronic gadgets. Now he is interested in computer activity.

He is very good in studies and also takes active part in all the extracurricular activities. He is very seriously preparing for his final exam. He has made up his mind that he will put all his effort in score as much as percentages possible in the exam. After the result depending upon the percentages he will decide in what line he should continue his further studies.

He has gathered lots of information various career related. He has kept lots of option for himself to take up after the higher secondary education. The first preference he has thought of civil engineering. As a civil engineer he prefers to work in northeast. He said that even if he gets job outside his own state he will work for around 10 years then come back to his state and start work for the development of his own place.

Usually he makes his own decision. Now and then he asks his friends for opinion before making decision. Parents encourage him to make his own decision by respecting his decision.

When asked about getting married and establishing own family he said, "I am not worried about getting married and establishing family. For now I have to work for secure job which will give me confidence to sustain my life." He prefers love marriage because he thinks that before living with a life partner one should know about the other. He wishes to have small family with 3 kids.

In the future he wants to be well known for his good work. His immediate plan is to pass the higher secondary well, give entrance exam for civil engineering and go for the study. He believes in undertaking a big task step by step.

Analysis

Here researcher analyses the data the researcher has collected from the respondent. The researcher makes use of check list matrix analyze the collected data. In the check list the researcher makes uses of code or labels to analyses the data. The concept labels were identified in the data and framed into the check list matrix. Each concept has been analysed separately and then formed a substantive hypotheses out of the analyses. The concepts are basically developed based on the objective of the study.

Check list Matrix

Concept label/names

Concept values

Decision making pattern of youth

Decision in daily life, decide independently, decides for self, opinion from parents, parents decides, consults uncle and aunty.

Future planning of youth

Plan for daily activities, activities depends, fixed plan, strong plan for future, what to do after studies, future plan.

Future carrier orientation of youth

Take engineering as his career, second option for career, not thought of career. I want to be but I don't know what are the studies required for the career. Choose career depending up HS result.

Future orientation of youth towards family

not thought of getting married and establish own family, marriage is not in mind, parents wish, now and then imagines, small and happy family in future.

Interest of youth

Besides studying interested in games and music, Interested in football and volleyball. Likes to read novels, interested in computer activities.

Efforts of youth for future

Sometime makes effort, career related knowledge.

Time perspective

Now and then thinks about future, though I like, I think afterwards it will be tough.

Understanding goal of youth

Clear short term goal, just does what she thinks need at that moment no long term goal.

Decision making pattern of youth

Youth is the unique stage of human growth and every stage of the growth people make decision for themselves for others. The decision making patter of youth no longer similar to their early stage. It is also can be true that the decision making patter of youth may change in later stage of life. The analysis of case narrative has shown that youth are mostly in influenced by their friends and class mates in daily life. Their decision on daily activities most of the time depends on others if not completed, at least partially. It clearly seen that youth of today are finding very difficult to decide independently. Many of the youth decide for themselves because they have seen people doing well in particular field. They not take much consideration what they exact like for themselves. The decision of youth today are influenced by the flowerily life style of few individual in the society without knowing the complete truth of them. Many youth decision is influenced by their parents and relatives. There are only few who are really making their decision independently. Again there are one more group of youth who has no choice but to make decision in a particular manner because of their life situation. Some are totally dependent on their parents for their decision though not many.

Future planning of youth

Planning is a process of making plan for doing or executing something. Planning is a part and parcel of successful lives. Again future planning is an act of planning for future. From the cash narratives it has been found that most of the youth do not plan for their daily activities. So, it will fare enough to state that a good many of youth today do plan the events of daily living. The activities or events in their life are actions that have emerge from the feelings. It will not be wrong to say that most of the youth's activities depend on their immediate feelings or needs or necessity. Thus, we can conclude that most of the youth do not really plan for future. It is also found that there are a few youth who do have future plan and are quite determine to achieve the plan. These few youth do plan out their activities and try to execute them. A very rare youth of today really have no absolutely plan for future. Again there are many youth who say they have plan but they do not do anything to execute or accomplish their work.

Future career orientation of youth

Future carrier orientation of youth is the thought or plan of taking a specific work as their career for their livelihood. It is found that most of the youth have similar types of career option. This implies that most of them hardly know about various types of career a youth can take up as their career to sustain their livelihood. Thus, it is quite clear that the future career orientation of youth is very much limited. There are many youth who thought of on only one career option. They never give a second thought different career. Again, there a few youth who are not sure what career they going to take up in future. There are a few categories of youth whose future careers are dependent on situation or luck.

Future orientation of youth towards family

Future orientation of youth towards family implies how prepared are the youth today to establish a family. Through the case narratives it is discovered that majority of the youth hardly think or do not think of getting married and establishing family. Getting married and raising children is never in their mind. There are a very few youth who think about or imagine of being married and having kids; have a small and happy family. Again, there are a countable handful of youth who wish to get married according to the wish of parents and left whole idea of marriage to their parents. Therefore, we can say that the future orientation of youth towards family life is very much low. It will correct to some extent to say that there is no future orientation of youth towards family.

Interest of youth

Interest is concept of liking or loving to do and never bore of that. After talking to some of the youth it is clear to certain extent that many of the youth of today still wondering or given a very less thought on what is their interest is. They are still figuring out what their interest is. But most of them have figure out their interest beside their daily studies. Some of the interests of youth today besides studying are games, music, watching movies, hanging out with friends, window shopping, reading novels, spending time in computer, mobile, face book, what's up etc. Again, it is also found that there is no direct connection or relation between their interest and the future career or plan they have, among most of the youth of today.

Efforts of youth for future

When it is said effort of youth for future it is implied the activities or tasks that are carried out which adds to the bigger picture of the future plan or goals the youth have. There are only a few youth who really make effort in to find out or to accomplish their future plan. A vast majority of the youth do just an average and below the average effort to meet the future according to their desire goals.

Time Perspective of youth

The time perspective of youth implies how so youth view time. It is found that most of youth of today hardly aware of time they are living through. Most of the youth do see the worth of time in their daily living which has led to mismanagement of time. Of course there are youth too who now and then think about their present and future time too, but they are very handful in number. There are also few youth who imagine their future and make changes in present life. This category of youth too is not very big in number.

Understanding goals of youth

There are basically two types of goals in life, namely short term goals and long term goals. It is found that a majority of the youth have short term goals but they vague idea or do not have much concept about the long term goals. Again, there are few numbers of youth who do have concept neither of short term goals nor the long term goals. They just do what they think best or needed at that moment without thinking the future or without thinking what comes next. At the end it can be concluded that youth have a low understanding of goals in terms of short and long goals.

Conclusion

Data analysis and interpretation is an essential part of any research study which lead the researcher to reach logical conclusion towards the end of the study. In this study the researcher tried to explain future orientation of youth by combining the quantitative and qualitative research methods. The quantitative data collected are analysed with the help of computer application and presented in the form of tables from which interpretation is obtained. The qualitative data is changed into concepts and constructs to frame a ground based theory on the view of the same by the school going youth.

CHAPTER FIVE

Introduction

In this chapter the researcher present the findings of the study. The findings are based on the data that researcher had analyzed in the previous chapter. The findings are associated with the researched, keeping in mind the outsider perspective the researcher made the following findings.

Major findings of the quantitative study

v. There is no one specific pattern of making decision among the school going youth.

v. The school going youth are not taught or do not given any orientation towards decision making pattern.

v. Majority of the youth are with limited future orientation.

v. More than (45.0 per cent) of school going youth follow some types of decision making pattern in their day to day life and for future.

v. Most of the youth have vision of future but in a limited manner.

v. 51.7 per cent of educated youth have directly or indirectly acquired orientation for their future towards planning or has a tendency to engage in thinking about future and involves expectation and hopes.

v. Majority of the youth cannot visualise or have their long term plan or fail to have long term future plan.

v. More than 48.3 per cent of school going youth could look into the future to some extent or able to forecast future to some distance or have future orientation.

v. 51.7 per cent and above educated youth have career orientation which they hope to pursue in life in the future.

v. Majority of the youth have limitation in the option for future career orientation.

v. Below the majority that is 48.3 per cent of school going youth have some type of family life orientation which they think they will apply in their life in the future.

v. It is found that there is an association between the decision making pattern and future planning of the schooling going youth.

v. The quantitative analysis shows that there is an association between decision making pattern and time perspective among the school going youth.

v. There is a relationship between age and future orientation of family life among the school going youth.

Major findings of the quantitative study

The future career orientations of youth are very much limited and have similar area of field for career option. There is a very minimum exploration among the youth for future career orientation. Most of them limit themselves to the ideas or words of parents, teachers and friends. They hardly explore the ocean they have within themselves. It is found that there is a future orientation towards career among youth but in less significances manner.

It is found that youth hardly make decision independently and purely by themselves. They most often rely on others for making any decision. Very often the decision of youth are influenced by friends and pressured from parents and teachers in various form. Many decisions of youth are based on immediate result. They also find difficult to make firm decision, meaning to say they are not certain about the decision they make.

From the study it is found that there is hardly any orientation of youth towards future family life. The idea of having family life is connected with the completion of career. It is found that most of the youth wish or will decide of getting married after getting a proper job. There is no deliberate effort made or preparation to live a married family life among the youth of today.

It is found that a very few youth could see into the future beyond 10 years. Most youth could look into the future of 5 years and not beyond. There are only a few who have the image of his or her concerning future role in the society. Majority of the youth do not have any future image of themselves. They just live the present with little focus of future one or two years which yet to come.

Suggestions

1. Reform in the school Education system: There is need of change in the school education system whereby the education system introduces new

way of imparting knowledge and result is visible not only in the report card but also in the day to day living experience. Children need to be helped in such way that they can visualise the consequence of their present behaviour.

2. Awareness for the parents and relatives: Parents and relative need to create and facilitate an environment for children whereby they could explore within themselves and also world around. Parents need to be encouraged to open the various windows for children and not restricting them to only one window to look their life.

3. Society need to have remedial approach: Low degree of future orientation among the youth of today is not the only problem of youth but it is the problem of whole nation as youth are considered as future of the nation. Therefore, nation needs to work out some common solution to the problem.

4. More research can be conducted to find the effective interventions to increase or to improve the future orientation among the youth.

5. There is a need of integration of youth policy and education policy whereby the policy help in undertaking various programme which can gradually help in holistic development school going youth; encourage them to have vision and orient them towards future.

Conclusion

Findings are the result of a research study. In this study, the researcher had put his effort through quantitative approach to study the future orientation of youth. The researcher has, after the analysis of the data collected; finding have been derived and framed into statistical derivatives.

The researcher had attempted to explore the understanding of the educated youth using the qualitative approach. The data was subjected to analysis process and the findings have been ensured coupled with the formation of hypotheses, ground based theory and suggestion.

CHAPTER SIX

Introduction

Integrated approach of research simply means combining quantitative and qualitative methods at all stages of the research study. Integrated approach relies on the presentation of facts through statistical results represented with numbers (quantitative) and words (qualitative).

When only one approach to research (qualitative or quantitative) is inadequate by itself to address the research problem, integrated research approach is the preferred research method. The combination of quantitative and qualitative data provides a more complete picture by noting trends and generalisations as well as in-depth knowledge of respondent's perspectives. One approach of research (qualitative or quantitative) might contradict the other form of approach of research (qualitative or quantitative)

The basic assumption of the integrated approach research is that the combination of quantitative and qualitative approaches provides a better understanding of research problem than one of the approaches alone. Integrated approach provides strengths that offset the weakness of both quantitative and qualitative approach research.

It is believed that quantitative approach research is weak in understanding the context or research setting in which people live. It is also said that the opinions of respondents are not heard in quantitative research. Furthermore, quantitative researcher's personal biases and interpretations are seldom discussed. On the other hand, qualitative approach research is seen as lacking because of the personal biases and interpretations by the researcher. For this reason the generalisation of findings is not possible. In qualitative approach research, usually a small number of subjects are studied. Consequently, generalising the findings to a large group becomes impractical.

Major Integration

In the quantitative research it is found that 51.7 per cent and above school going youth have future career orientation which they hope to pursue in life in the future. But the majority of the youth have limitation in the option for future career orientation. On the other hand from the ground based theory it has been analysed that the future career orientations of youth are very much limited and have similar area of field for career option. There is a very minimum exploration among the youth for future career orientation. Most of them have limited themselves to the ideas or words of parents, teachers and friends. They hardly explore the ocean they have within themselves. It is found that there is a future orientation towards career among youth but in less significances manner. Now, the integration of qualitative and qualitative findings leads to the conclusion that there is no doubt about having future career orientation among the school going youth today but majority of the youth are more of restricted vision.

Again, the qualitative finding shows that there is no one specific pattern of making decision among the school going youth. The school going youth are not taught or not given any orientation towards decision making pattern. More than (45.0 per cent) of school going youth follow some type of decision making pattern in their day to day life and for future. On the other hand the analysis of ground based theory show that youths hardly make decision independently and purely. They most often rely on other for making any decision. Very often the decision of youth are influenced by friends and pressured from parents and teachers in various form. Many decisions of youth are based on immediate result. They also find difficult to make firm decision, meaning to say they are not certain about the decision they make. Thus, integration of qualitative and quantitative finding leads to the wrapping up that youth of today have a pattern of making decision for future which does not consist of standardised pattern of decision making. Most of the school going youth of today have future orientation towards decision making pattern but in limited manner. The orientation towards decision making pattern of present youth covers only a short term visualization of future.

One more finding of qualitative study shows that below the average of school going youth have future orientation towards family life. It is also found that there is a significant relationship between age and future orientation of family life among the educated youth of today. On the other hand the analysis of the ground based theory shows that there is hardly any orientation of youth towards future family life. The idea of having family life is connected with the completion of career. It is found that most of the youth have a very vague concept of establishing family after getting a proper career. There is no deliberate effort made or preparation to live a married family life among the youth of today. Hence, the integration of the qualitative and quantitative finding leads to the termination that the future orientation towards family life among the school going youth of today is very much low or present in very regrettable manner.

Overall finding of the integrated research is that the majority of the educated youth of today able to look into the future and the images individuals hold concerning their future, able to foresee the future implications of their present behaviour. They understand how their present task-engagement is meaningfully related to desired future events and how their present behaviour serves the attainment of those future events. They have tendency to engage in thinking about the future and involves expectations, hopes, and fears. There is a future orientation among the educated youth but of more restricted vision. The willingness to postpone or forego pleasures for a future reward or a tolerance of present discomfort for the hope of future compensation is less in majority of the educated youth.

Therefore, today most of the youth are having difficulties in dreaming future dreams and the future orientation toward decision making; career, family life, time perspective etc. are in stack and need some intervention at the early stage of their life as a way out to the problem.

CHAPTER SEVEN

Summary

The study is based, on the interest of the researcher to understand future orientation of school going youth with reference to town and contribute in bringing about change in orientation system and development in the society.

There are studies done on the orientation towards future but the researcher has found no such study which has totally focused on school going youth as the contributing factor in the dynamics of change of the society.

The researcher has used integrated approach of social science research in order to attain a comprehensive understanding of the research study complementing the quantitative and qualitative approach all across the study process.

The results and inferences of the subject of study are done through the technique of triangulation convergence research design. The sampling size used for the quantitative data is 60, through the use of questionnaires as the tool for collecting data. The unstructured in depth interview is used as a tool to collect the data for the qualitative approach.

Chapter I of the research study deals with the introduction of the research where in the background of the study and the significance of the study is laid out. Chapter II reviews the conceptualization of the study which is actually the literature related to the study either from books, websites, newspapers, journals, articles, magazines and other sources. Chapter III explains the research methodology. Chapter IV is the case narratives where the qualitative data is set out into checklist matrices for analysis. Chapter V is the analysis and interpretation of the collected data. The analysis and interpretation is done with the help of the two approaches as result of comparing and contrasting the result of the approaches: compare and con-relate the two data sets and validate or expand the results of both the approaches. Chapter VI is the presentation of the findings of the research based on the analyzed data and Chapter VII gives the summary of

• 43 •

the entire research.

Conclusion

A study on the future orientation of school going youth with reference to Jorhat town, Assam was a small attempt to understand the degree of future orientation of youth towards their future, especially towards their future family life, decision for future and future career. Youth, is a time when impulsivity and sensation seeking, combined with a lack of orientation toward future consequences, are likely to be pronounced. Future orientation, or the image individuals have of the future, provides the foundation for setting goals and planning, and therefore is considered an important youth developmental task.

Based on the results, future orientation is unpredictable that can serve as both a risk and protective factor. Attention to these findings is likely to result in enhanced prevention and intervention programming with youth. In terms of prevention programming, future planning components will be useful for all youth. In terms of intervention, providing mentors or specialized attention to youth with a low future orientation may also result in more positive outcomes.

Higher secondary education serves as a link between the elementary and higher education, and plays a very vital role in this respect. A youth's future can depend a lot on the type of education she or he receives at the secondary level. Apart from grounding the roots of education of a youth, higher secondary education can be instrumental in shaping and directing a youth to a bright future. The higher secondary level education includes youth between the age group 14 – 25 years, studying in classes IX-X leading to higher secondary classes of XI and XII. 'The future of the nation is in the hands of our young people. They will give it the right direction if they are the person who orient well in this stage of life and have vision for his or her life'(youth vision, 2004). Low scale of future orientation among the youth of today is not the only problem of youth but it is the problem of whole society as youth are considered as future of the nation. Therefore, society needs to work out some common solution to the problem. From the perspective of social worker, to bring about this change in the future orientation among the young social work intervention research will be the best to start as a solution to the problem.

Bibliography

Books

1. Arlene Harder, MFT. (2008). *Ask yourself question and change your life.* Mumbai-400023: Published in India by Embassy book distributors.
2. D.K. Lal Das. (2013). *Approaches to social science Research Methods.* Published by New Royal Book Company, Lucknow, India.
3. Devasia Puthiaparambil, SSP. (2005) *Positive Attitudes for Life.* Mumbai, Bandra and published by saint Pauls.
4. John Adair. (1985). *Effective Decision Making.* New Delhi-110002: Printed in India by Ahad Enterprise.
5. John Rarankimalil. (2003). *The way to Success and Happiness.* New Delhi-110060. Published by Sacio Publication Pvt. Ltd.
6. Mammen Mathew, ed. (2013) *Manorama Yearbook.* Printed and published from Malayala Manorama press, Kottayam-686001.
7. Marcus Buckingham & Donald O. Clifton, Ph.D. (2001). *Now, Discover Your Strengths.* New York, NY 10020. Published by the free press, a Division of Simon & Schuster Inc.
8. Morgan, C.T. King, R.A., Weisz, J.R. & Schopler, J. (2008). *Introduction to Psychology.* New Delhi-110032: Tata Mctraw-Hills publishing Company Limited.
9. Rob Yeung. (2002). *The ten career commandments.* Published by better yourself books.
10. Vattathara, T., & Michael, B. (2004). *Youth vision.* Guwahati: Don Bosco Institute Publication.

Websites

1. http://www.businessdictionary.com/definition/career.html
2. http://kalyan-city.blogspot.com/2011/08/what-is-decision-making-meaning.html
3. http://www.unesco.org/new/en/social-and-human-sciences/themes/youth/youth-definition/
4. http://futureorientation.net/2010/07/29/what-is-organizational-future-orientation/
5. http://link.springer.com/article/10.1007%2FBF02087616#page-2

6. http://www.temple.edu/tunl/publications/documents/
   Age_Diff_in_Future_Orientation_and_Delay_Discounting_CD.pdf
7. http://undesadspd.org/Youth.aspx
8. facebook.com/UN4Youth
9. twitter.com/UN4Youth

Report
(2011). *The UN Youth Agenda.*